Diet recommendations for TCM - Kidney - Qi is not fixed

Please check these recommendations always with a nutrition consultant, therapist, doctor or dietician. The recipes and the list of ingredients are supporting the conventional medical therapy.
The calorie disclosures of fresh ingredients (fruit and vegetables) vary according to quality and time of harvest. The contents were checked by a dietician and a nutrition consultant for the Traditional Chinese Medicine (TCM).

Author:
©2019 Josef Miligui
www.ebns.at

AF205131

Source:
The lists are created from the EBNS database for nutritional counseling. The database is used by dietitians, therapists and doctors for advising the patient / client.

Literature:
The specialist literature and the training documents of the German and Austrian dietary and traditional Chinese medicine serve as a knowledge base. We have used the documents as a basis of knowledge, adapted it to our experience and completed them.
http://di-book.com

Production and publishing:
BoD – Books on Demand, Norderstedt
ISBN: 9783746097459

Diet recommendations for TCM - Kidney - Qi is not fixed

1 Treatment strategy

Strengthen and stabilize kidneys.
Hot NO, warm and neutral YES, refreshing LITTLE (except sour YES), cold NO.

2 Avoid

Everything that dehydrates !!!, sugar, cucumbers, tomatoes, coffee ....

3   Breakfast

4   Snack

5   Lunch

6   Afternoon

7   Dinner

8 Any time

9 Recipes

(rec.) = You can use more.
(little) = You should use less than specified
(omit) = omit.

9.1 8 treasures of rice

Strengthens kidney and bladder, builds up Qi, strengthens the spleen, repels moisture, reduces internal heat, prevents cancer, builds heart, calms nerves.
Cooking time approx. 1 hour
Calories p. portion: 223
4 portions

Quantity of ingredients:
Lily bulbs 1 table spoon / 5g. () - cool - sweet, bitter .... *
Longane 1 table spoon / 5g. (little) - warm - sweet... *
King Solomon's-seal 1 table spoon / 5g. () - neutral - sweet, bitter .... *
Yam root, yam root tuber 1 table spoon / 5g. () - neutral - sweet .... *
Coix (seeds) YiYi Ren 1 table spoon / 5g. (yes) - cool - sweet, neutral............ *
Rice wild (nature rice) 1 1/2 cups / 240g. (rec.) - neutral - sweet, bitter .... metal
Water 8-10 cups / 800g. (yes) - cool - salty..earth

Cooking instructions:
Each one 1 tbsp: Bai He, Longan, Yu Zhu, Da Zao, Shan Yao, Lian Mi, Yi Yi Ren, Qian Shi
Add hot water and soak for about 30 minutes. Then add 1 - 2 cups of rice (normal) and simmer for 1/2 to 1 hour until the rice is very soft. Or: Cook for about 3 hours with the herbs a congee. Then the herbs do not have to be soaked.

9.2 Basic recipe for a beef broth (clear)

Strengthens Qi and Yang, is very warming.
Cooking time approx. 4-8 hours
Calories p. portion: 114
10 portions
Allergens: O

Quantity of ingredients:
Beef soup meat 1,1 lbs / 500g. () - warm - sweet.......................................earth
Beef meatbones 5/8 oz / 200g. (little) - warm - sweet ....earth
Vinegar (Red wine vinegar) 1 dash / 3g. (little) - warm - sour, bitter .... wood
Juniper berry 8 pieces / 6g. (omit) - warm - sweet, acrid, bitter....................fire

Rosemary 1 pinch / 1g. (omit) - warm - bitter ....fire
Carrot 3 pieces / 210g. (yes) - neutral - sweet ....earth
Parsnip 2 pieces / 300g. (rec.) - cool - bitter..fire
Leek 1 piece / 200g. (rec.) - warm - acrid...metal
Ginger fresh 1/2 teaspoon / 5g. (omit) - warm - acrid..............................metal
Lovage 1 stem / 15g. (omit) - warm - acrid, bitter......................................metal
Clove 2 pieces / 2g. (rec.) - warm - acrid..metal
Pimento 6 pieces / 12g. (omit) - hot - acrid...metal
Anise (Common Fennel) 2 pieces / 1g. (little) - warm - acrid.....................earth
Salt 1 teaspoon / 5g. (yes) - cold - salty ....water
Water 3,3 lbs / 1300g. (yes) - cool - salty...earth

Cooking instructions:
Heat water, a dash of red wine vinegar, some juniper berries, a little
rosemary, bones and meat till it boils; add carrot, parsnip, leek, ginger,
lovage, clove, allspice, star anise and a little salt; simmer for 4-8 hours
then strain.
Refrigerate for later use.

9.3   Basic recipe for a chicken broth worming

Strengthens Qi and blood, is very warm.
Cooking time approx. 2-3 hours
Calories p. portion: 90
9 portions
Allergens: L

Quantity of ingredients:
Chicken meat 1/2 piece / 600g. (little) - warm - sweet.............................. wood
Carrot 2 pieces / 150g. (yes) - neutral - sweet ....earth
Leek 1 stick / 45g. (rec.) - warm - acrid ....metal
Celery root 1 piece / 500g. (rec.) - cool - sweet..earth
Ginger fresh 2 slices / 2g. (omit) - warm - acrid..metal
Juniper berry 1 teaspoon / 3g. (omit) - warm - sweet, acrid, bitter ....fire
Bay leaf 3 pieces / 2g. () - warm - acrid..metal
Water 4 cup / 900g. (yes) - cool - salty..earth

Cooking instructions:
Remove chicken parts from fat. Place chicken pieces in a saucepan
with hot water and heat till it boils briefly, skimming any resulting foam.
Add coarsely chopped vegetables and all spices and cook over medium
heat for 2 to 3 hours. Strain the finished soup. Throw away vegetables
and bones.
Tip: If you want to use the meat as a soup insert, take out after 45
minutes and return only the bones in the soup. Refrigerate for later use.

9.4 Basic recipe for a reissue soup (Congee)

Warms the stomach and spleen, harmonizes the intestine, forces Qi, reduces moisture.
Cooking time approx. 2-4 hours
Calories p. portion: 140
3 portions

Quantity of ingredients:
Rice variety any 1 cup / 120g. (yes) - warm - sweet..................................metal
Water 6 cups / 700g. (yes) - cool - salty...earth

Cooking instructions:
Cook rice and water in a ratio of about 1: 6. The amount of water determines the thickness of the mash (matter of taste).
Put the rice in a saucepan with a heavy lid. It is important to simmer the rice after a short boil on the slightest flame, otherwise it burns.
Boil the rice for 2-4 hours. The longer it cooks, the more it strengthens. If you want to eat the dish for breakfast, you can put the rice on just before bedtime.
To be on the safe side, you should first check the behavior of your pot and cooker under observation for a similar amount of time, so that nothing burns.
Refrigerate for later use.

9.5 Basic recipe for a vegetable soup, nutritious

Strengthens spleen and lung, regulates Qi flow, builds up Qi, dries out, passes downwardly, strengthens stomach Qi.
Cooking time approx. 2-3 hours
Calories p. portion: 48
5 portions
Allergens: L

Quantity of ingredients:
Olive oil 1 table spoon / 4g. (yes) - cool - sweet..earth
Onion white 1 piece / 60g. (yes) - warm - acrid ....metal
Carrot 3 pieces / 200g. (yes) - neutral - sweet ....earth
Parsnip 3/8 lbs - 6oz / 150g. (rec.) - cool - bitter ....fire
Celery root 1 cup / 100g. (rec.) - cool - sweet ....earth
Ginger fresh 1/2 teaspoon / 2g. (omit) - warm - acrid..............................metal
Lemon 1/2 piece / 25g. (omit) - cold - sour...wood
Juniper berry 6 pieces / 6g. (omit) - warm - sweet, acrid, bitter....................fire
Thyme dried 1 pinch / 1g. () - warm - bitter ....metal
Lovage 1 table spoon / 3g. (omit) - warm - acrid, bitter ....metal

Bay leaf 2 leaves / 1g. () - warm - acrid.. metal
Salt 1 pinch / 1g. (yes) - cold - salty .... water
Water 3 cups / 650g. (yes) - cool - salty ....earth

Cooking instructions:
Cut the vegetables into cubes.
Heat oil in hot pot, fry shortly onions and vegetables.
Add cold water, then add ginger, bay leaf and lemon juice.
Season with juniper, thyme and lovage. Cover for 2 - 3 hours on a low heat and simmer.
The used vegetables should be thrown away.
The basic recipe serves as a soup base and to refine vegetables, legumes or cereals.
If you want to eat vegetable soup immediately, add the desired vegetables half an hour before.
Refrigerate for later use.

9.6   Beef soup with carrots, leeks, bay leaves

Strengthens spleen Qi, strengthens blood and Qi, moisturizes, relaxes, builds up Qi, spreads, strengthens spleen and liver, regulates Qi flow, strengthens stomach Qi.
Cooking time approx. 2-3 hours
Calories p. portion: 194
5 portions

Quantity of ingredients:
Beef meat 1 lbs / 500g. (little) - warm - sweet ....earth
Carrot 2 pieces / 200g. (yes) - neutral - sweet ....earth
Leek 1/2 piece / 150g. (rec.) - warm - acrid... metal
Bay leaf 3 leaves / 1g. () - warm - acrid... metal
Corn Grease (Polenta) 1 table spoon / 10g. (rec.) - neutral - sweet...........earth
Water 2 cup / 450g. (yes) - cool - salty..earth
Salt 1 pinch / 0,5g. (yes) - cold - salty .... water

Cooking instructions:
In a saucepan with water (enough to cover the meat), add beef soup meat or leg slice and simmer for a moment; then pour off the broth, rinse the meat with hot water (this will save you from foaming), clean the pot and put the meat in hot water again; add chopped carrot, leek, corn and bay leaf; simmer until the meat is cooked.

9.7   Black-eyed beans stew

Strengthens spleen and kidney, is very nutritious, warms the stomach and spleen, harmonizes the intestine, forces Qi, strengthens stomach and kidney, strengthens spleen and kidney.
Cooking time approx. 20 min
Calories p. portion: 140
5 portions

Quantity of ingredients:
Black-eyed peas 1 cup / 100g. (yes) - neutral - sweet, acrid.................... water
Rice variety any 1 1/2 cups / 200g. (yes) - warm - sweet.......................... metal
Water 10 cups / 1000g. (yes) - cool - salty...earth

Cooking instructions:
Soak the beans overnight and strain.

In a ratio of 1: 2, simmer the beans together with the rice in the Water. Depending on how hot the flame is and how
thin the dish should be, more water must be added.

Variation: Add vegetables fried in oil, such as carrots, celery tubers, onions or leeks.

9.8   Blueberry puree

Keeps fluids and essence, forces liver and kidneys, forces blood, forces eyesight, warms spleen- and kidney-Yang, directs upwards, warms the stomach and spleen, promotes blood circulation and conduction flow, relieves cold-sickness and pain..
Cooking time approx. 10 min
Calories p. portion: 10
1 portion

Quantity of ingredients:
Blueberry 1/2 oz / 20g. (rec.) - cool - sweet, sour .... wood
Cinnamon ground 1 pinch / 0,1g. (rec.) - hot - acrid, sweet.................*
Clove 1 piece / 1g. (rec.) - warm - acrid .... metal
Water 1 cup / 250g. (yes) - cool - salty...earth

Cooking instructions:
Boil blueberries with cinnamon and clove in water for 10 minutes.
Remove the cinnamon and clove. Puree. Sweet as desired.

9.9 Breakfast - Rice with fruits

Harmonizes the intestine, forces Qi, reduces moisture, preserves the fluids, contracts, nourishes fluids, moistens dryness in the lungs, produces humors, moisturizes intestines, cools inner heat.
Cooking time approx. 10 min - 3 hours
Calories p. portion: 231
3 portions
Allergens: GHO

Quantity of ingredients:
Basic recipe for a rice soup (Congee) 6 cups / 500g. (rec.) - neutral - sweet... *
Cow's milk (3.5% fat) 1/2 to 1 cup / 80g. (little) - neutral - sweet...............earth
Honey 1 table spoon / 10g. (little) - cold - sweet ....earth
Butter organic 1 table spoon / 15g. (yes) - neutral - sweet.........................earth
Dates dried 1 table spoon / 15g. (little) - warm - sweet ....earth
Fig 1 table spoon / 15g. (yes) - warm - sweet ....earth
Apple (sour) 1 piece / 200g. (yes) - cool - sour .... wood
Hazelnuts 1/2 teaspoon / 5g. (yes) - neutral - sweet.................................earth
Almond 1/2 teaspoon / 5g. (yes) - neutral - sweet.....................................earth
Cinnamon ground 1 pinch / 1g. (rec.) - hot - acrid, sweet................................. *

Cooking instructions:
Cook rice congee according to basic recipe or use pre-cooked.
Make it with the milk more fluid, and sweet with honey.
Fry the fruits and nuts in butter and mix with the finished rice soup, add chopped dates, figs and the apple.

9.10 Carrot and rice gruel soup

Warms the stomach and spleen, harmonizes the intestine, forces Qi, reduces moisture, strengthens spleen and liver, regulates Qi flow, moisturizes, relaxes, builds up Qi, spreads.
Cooking time approx. 10 min
Calories p. portion: 101
1 portion

Quantity of ingredients:
Basic recipe for a rice soup (Congee) 1 cup / 120g. (rec.) - neutral - sweet..... *
Carrot 2 pieces / 100g. (yes) - neutral - sweet ....earth
Salt 1 teaspoon / 4g. (yes) - cold - salty .... water

Cooking instructions:
Peel and grate carrots. Heat the rice soup (according to the basic recipe) till it boils and add the grated carrots and salt. Cook for 10 minutes.

9.11 Celery juice

Strengthens stomach Qi, moisturizes, relaxes, builds up Qi, spreads.
Cooking time approx. 5 min
Calories p. portion: 33
1 portion
Allergens: L

Quantity of ingredients:
Celery root 1/2 piece / 200g. (rec.) - cool - sweet.....................................earth
Water 1 cup / 120g. (yes) - cool - salty...earth
Salt 1 pinch / 0,5g. (yes) - cold - salty ....water

Cooking instructions:
Peel celeriac and cut into pieces and juice. Mix with water and salt as needed.

9.12 Chicken soup with angelica root and buckthorn fruit

Strengthens spleen and nourishes the blood and Yin of the liver, forces Qi and blood, is very warming.
Cooking time approx. 1 1/2 hours
Calories p. portion: 77
3 portions
Allergens: LO

Quantity of ingredients:
Basic recipe for a chicken soup (warming) 2 cup / 500g. () - warm - * .... *
Bocksdorn fruits (Lycii, goji berry dried 1/8 lbs - 2oz / 50g. () - cool - .... wood

Cooking instructions:
When you cook chicken broth according to basic recipes add angelica root and willowberry fruits in the last 40 minutes.

Ingestion: Drink 2-3 cups of broth daily.

9.13 Compote from blueberries

Keeps fluids and essence, forces liver and kidneys, forces blood, forces eyesight, reduces internal heat, produces humors, leads Qi down.
Cooking time approx. 10 min
Calories p. portion: 49
1 portion

Quantity of ingredients:
Blueberry 1/4 lbs - 4oz / 100g. (rec.) - cool - sweet, sour .... wood
Water 1 cup / 120g. (yes) - cool - salty .... earth
Cinnamon ground 1 pinch / 0,1g. (rec.) - hot - acrid, sweet .... *
Lemon peel 1 pinch / 1g. (rec.) - cool - bitter .... fire
Sugar cane sugar 1 teaspoon / 3g. (little) - cool - sweet .... earth

Cooking instructions:
Cook the blueberries gently and sprinkle with sugar, cinnamon and grated lemon zest.

9.14 Compote from cherries

Moisturizes liver and kidney, forces middle, reduces blood congestion, reduces internal heat, warms the stomach and spleen, promotes blood circulation and conduction flow, relieves cold-sickness and pain.
Cooking time approx. 10 min
Calories p. portion: 32
2 portions

Quantity of ingredients:
Cherry 1/4 lbs - 4oz / 100g. (rec.) - warm - sweet, sour .... earth
Water 1 1/2 cups / 240g. (yes) - cool - salty .... earth
Cinnamon ground 1 pinch / 0,2g. (rec.) - hot - acrid, sweet .... *

Cooking instructions:
Cook the cherries in the water until soft. Sprinkle with a little cinnamon.

9.15 Grape compote

Relaxes, builds up Qi, spreads, moisten the lungs and large intestine.
Cooking time approx. 10 min
Calories p. portion: 128
1 portion
Allergens: H

Quantity of ingredients:
Grapes red 3/8 lbs - 6oz / 150g. (rec.) - cool - sweet ....earth
Water 4 table spoons / 30g. (yes) - cool - salty ....earth
Almond 1 teaspoon / 3g. (yes) - neutral - sweet...earth

Cooking instructions:
Remove the grapes from the stems, wash thoroughly in warm water and drain. Halve the grapes (remove the seeds for babies). In a small saucepan, heat 4 tablespoons of water with the grapes and the grated almonds till it boils. Cook over low heat for about 3 minutes, then chill. (For babies lukewarm).

9.16 Grape juice (fresh, homemade)

Moisturizes, relaxes, builds up Qi, spreads.
Cooking time approx. 15 min
Calories p. portion: 73
2 portions

Quantity of ingredients:
Grapes white 7/8 lbs / 200g. (rec.) - neutral - sweet, sour ....earth

Cooking instructions:
For about 200 ml of juice, pluck 400 g of white grapes (alternatively berries or stone fruit) from the stalk, wash thoroughly, drain and halve. Fill in the sieve insert of the pressure cooker. On the bottom of the pot pour about 2 cm high water, stack the cross, the juice bowl (accessories) and the sieve with the grapes on top of each other. Close the pot and juice the grapes for about 12 minutes.

9.17 Hot water with grape juice

Juice or blood deficiency
Cooking time approx. 5 min
Calories p. portion: 87
1 portion

Quantity of ingredients:
Grape juice red 1 cup / 120g. (rec.) - neutral - sweet, sour ....earth
Water 1/2 cup / 60g. (yes) - cool - salty..earth

Cooking instructions:
Heat the water till it boils and add it to the grape juice.

9.18 Kohlrabi Potatoes mash

Moves Qi and blood, reduces moisture, forces Qi, forces spleen, relieves inflammation, moisturizes, relaxes, builds up Qi, spreads, forces kidney Jing.
Cooking time approx. 25 min
Calories p. portion: 278
1 portion
Allergens: CG

Quantity of ingredients:
Kohlrabi 1/2 piece / 150g. (yes) - neutral - acrid, sweet ....earth
Potato 1/4 lbs - 4oz / 100g. (yes) - neutral - sweet....................................earth
Butter organic 1 table spoon / 10g. (yes) - neutral - sweet.........................earth
Chicken yolk 1 piece / 25g. (rec.) - neutral - sweet ....earth

Cooking instructions:
Remove the kohlrabi leaves, wash the tuber and tender leaves and the potatoes thoroughly. Peel the kohlrabi and potatoes, cut into cubes about 1 cm in size. Melt half the butter in a small saucepan, add the kohlrabi and the potatoes and fry in it. Steam with 2 tablespoons of water in a closed saucepan over low heat for about 15 minutes. Meanwhile, free the tenderest kohlrabi leaves from the stems and chop very finely. In total, at most 2 tablespoons of leaf pieces should be used. Add this to the vegetables about 5 minutes before the end of the cooking time. Stir in the egg yolk and bring to the boil again. Put the vegetables in a plate and mix with the remaining butter and egg yolk. (Crush for the baby with a fork.)

9.19 Kuzu soup in the morning

Moisturizes, relaxes, builds up Qi, spreads, forces stomach, harmonizes middle, reduces internal heat, detoxifies, softens, passes downwardly.
Cooking time approx. 5 min
Calories p. portion: 12
1 portion
Allergens: E

Quantity of ingredients:
Water 1 cup / 250g. (yes) - cool - salty...earth
Soy sauce 1 dash / 2g. (omit) - cold - salty ....water
Umeboshi paste 1 knife tip / 2g. () - warm - sour..water

Cooking instructions:

Mix Kuzu with cold water and heat till it boils while stirring. Once it is glassy, remove from heat and let cool. Season
with Tamari and Umeboshipaste or crushed umeboshi plums

There is always the possibility to support your stomach and intestines with this recipe, taken before the right breakfast.
A morning cure for stomach and mucous membranes. Fix the base balance.

9.20 Lentils and rice stew

Strengthens spleen and liver, regulates Qi flow, moisturizes, relaxes, builds up Qi, spreads, warms the stomach and spleen, harmonizes the intestine, forces Qi, reduces moisture, brings the liver Qi in motion, cools heat.
Cooking time approx. 25 min
Calories p. portion: 232
3 portions
Allergens: LNO

Quantity of ingredients:

Lentils 1/4 lbs - 4oz / 100g. (yes) - neutral - sweet, sour .... water
Water 5 cups / 500g. (yes) - cool - salty .... earth
Rice variety any 1 cup / 120g. (yes) - warm - sweet .... metal
Sesame oil 1 table spoon / 10g. (yes) - cool - sweet .... earth
Carrot 2 pieces / 150g. (yes) - neutral - sweet .... earth
Celery sticks 2 rods / 20g. (rec.) - cool - sweet .... earth
Cumin (Caraway seed) 1 pinch / 0,2g. (little) - warm - acrid .... metal
Salt 1 pinch / 0,5g. (yes) - cold - salty .... water
Vinegar (Apple vinegar) 1 dash / 2g. (little) - warm - sour, bitter .... wood
Parsley 2 table spoons / 18g. (rec.) - warm - bitter .... wood

Cooking instructions:

Soak the dry lentils the day before.
Heat sesame oil in a hot pot; cut carrot and celery into small pieces and sauté; add rice, a pinch of cumin and lentils and heat till it boils.
If the lenses are soft, add salt; season with a little vinegar and garnish with parsley.

Variant: In summer you can omit the cumin and add fresh green peas, Chinese cabbage or celery.

9.21 Spinach flan with milk

Forces Qi, forces spleen, relieves inflammation, moisturizes, relaxes, builds up Qi, spreads, forces blood, Yin and Jing, nourishes Yin, moisturizes in case of internal dryness, nourishes blood and Yi, forces Zang-organs.
Cooking time approx. 1 min
Calories p. portion: 250
1 portion
Allergens: ACG

Quantity of ingredients:
Potato 1/4 lbs - 4oz / 100g. (yes) - neutral - sweet......................................earth
Spinach 1/8 lbs - 2oz / 50g. (rec.) - cool - sweet, rough ....earth
Chicken egg 1 piece / 65g. (rec.) - neutral - sweet....................................earth
Breadcrumbs (wheat bread) 1 teaspoon / 3g. (rec.) - cool - sweet, salty .. wood
Cow's milk (3.5% fat) 6 table spoons / 50g. (little) - neutral - sweet ....earth
Crème fraiche cheese 1 teaspoon / 3g. (yes) - neutral - sweet.................earth
Butter organic 1 teaspoon / 3g. (yes) - neutral - sweet.............................earth

Cooking instructions:
Wash the potatoes and cook with a little water in about 20 minutes.
Heat the water till it boils. Clean the fresh spinach and add to the boiling water (the frozen unfreeze), bring to the boil again and boil for about 2 minutes. Drain the spinach and puree.
Peel the potatoes and squeeze them through the potato press or crush them with the potato masher.
Mix with the spinach, egg and breadcrumbs.
Grease a small, refractory form (about 300 ml) with the butter and pour in the vegetable musk. Put the dish in a saucepan and pour enough water into the saucepan that the dish is two-thirds in a water bath.
Cover and simmer for 15 minutes over medium heat.
Heat the milk with the creme fraiche.
Put the spinach flan on a plate and pour the milk over it.

9.22 Red grape juice with egg yolk

Tonifies Yin and Qi, brings blood into motion, exudes moisture, detoxifying.
Cooking time approx. 5 min
Calories p. portion: 271
1 portion
Allergens: C

Quantity of ingredients:
Grape juice red 1 cup / 250g. (rec.) - neutral - sweet, sour ....earth
Chicken yolk 1 piece / 25g. (rec.) - neutral - sweet ....earth

Cooking instructions:
Whisk egg yolks in grape juice.

9.23 Rice congee with carrots and fennel

Nutritious builds up Qi, forces the digestive functions.
Cooking time approx. 2 hours and more
Calories p. portion: 131
3 portions
Allergens: G

Quantity of ingredients:
Basic recipe for a rice soup (Congee) 2 cup / 500g. (rec.) - neutral - sweet..... *
Carrot 2 pieces / 100g. (yes) - neutral - sweet ....earth
Fennel 1 piece / 250g. (yes) - warm - sweet, little acrid ....earth
Butter organic 1 teaspoon / 3g. (yes) - neutral - sweet..............................earth
Cardamom 1/2 teaspoon / 1g. () - warm - acrid...metal

Cooking instructions:
Cook rice congee according to basic recipe.
Clean and cut carrots and fennel.

When carrots and fennel are cooked from the beginning, they serve
wholesomeness. If added shortly before the end of the cooking time,
taste and vitamins are retained.

Refine with butter and cardamom before serving.

9.24 Rice congee with crushed walnuts

Nourishing and slightly warming, warms the middle, builds up Qi, warms
the stomach and spleen, harmonizes the intestine, forces Qi, reduces
moisture.
Cooking time approx. 2 hours and more
Calories p. portion: 406
2 portions
Allergens: H

Quantity of ingredients:
Basic recipe for a rice soup (Congee) 4 cups / 500g. (rec.) - neutral - sweet... *
Sugar cane sugar 2 table spoons / 20g. (little) - cool - sweet.....................earth
Walnuts 1 cup / 70g. (yes) - warm - sweet ....earth
Cinnamon ground 1 pinch / 0,2g. (rec.) - hot - acrid, sweet........................... *

Cooking instructions:
Cook the basic recipe for rice soup (congee)
Note: The crushed walnuts can be cooked from the beginning.
Variation: Refine with sweet or spicy ingredients as you like. In particular, cinnamon, cloves, and ginger increase the warming effect and wholesomeness.

9.25 Rice congee with dried fruit

Warms the stomach and spleen, harmonizes the intestine, forces Qi, reduces moisture, nourishes blood and Yi, harmonizes lungs Qi, strengthens Qi and kidney Jing, moisturizes, relaxes, builds up Qi, spreads.
Cooking time approx. 10 min
Calories p. portion: 210
2 portions
Allergens: GO

Quantity of ingredients:
Basic recipe for a rice soup (Congee) 4 cups / 500g. (rec.) - neutral - sweet... *
Butter organic 1/2 teaspoon / 5g. (yes) - neutral - sweet...........................earth
Apricot dried 6 table spoons / 50g. () - warm - sweet ....earth
Water 1/2 cup / 50g. (yes) - cool - salty...earth
Maple syrup 1 dash / 3g. (yes) - cool - sweet..earth

Cooking instructions:
Cook rice congee according to basic recipe.

Melt a small amount of butter over a low heat and briefly fry small dried fruit with 1/2 cup of water. Add the amount of rice porridge desired for the meal and heat. Serve hot and sweeten with maple syrup if necessary.
Variant: In addition, fresh fruit with braise.

9.26 Rice congee with honey pear and black sesame

Especially good in kidney Yin deficiency, moisturizes lungs, cools heat, reduces lung mucus, produces humors, moisturizes, relaxes, builds up Qi, spreads, moisturizes intestines, nourishes Yin.
Cooking time approx. 10 min - 3 hours
Calories p. portion: 158
2 portions
Allergens: N

Quantity of ingredients:
Basic recipe ... (Congee) 1 1/2 cups / 240g. (rec.) - neutral - sweet................ *
Pear 2 pieces / 300g. (yes) - cool - sweet, sour ....earth

Cooking instructions:
Cook rice congee according to basic recipe.
Fill pot with 3 cm of water and heat till it boils. Quarter the pears (with the skin and seeds) and simmer them covered with black sesame for 10 minutes. Mix with the rice.

9.27 Rice congee with mung beans

Warms the stomach and spleen, harmonizes the intestine, forces Qi, reduces moisture, reduces heat, softens, passes downwardly, moisturizes, laxative, antiparasitic.
Cooking time approx. 2 hours
Calories p. portion: 424
2 portions

Quantity of ingredients:
Basic recipe for a rice soup (Congee) 4 cups / 500g. (rec.) - neutral - sweet... *
Mung bean 1/2 cup / 50g. (rec.) - cool - sweet, salty................................ water
Rapeseed oil 2 table spoons / 20g. (yes) - neutral - sweet........................earth

Cooking instructions:
Soak the mung beans the day before and strain. Cook the rice according to the basic recipe and cook the mung beans with the rice. Finally, add fresh herbs and a dash of high-quality cold-pressed oil.

9.28 Rice dulse soup

Strengthens spleen and liver, regulates Qi flow, relaxes, builds up Qi, spreads, dries out, passes downwardly, strengthens stomach Qi, warms the stomach and spleen, harmonizes the intestine, forces Qi, reduces moisture.
Cooking time approx. 5 min
Calories p. portion: 190
2 portions
Allergens: L

Quantity of ingredients:
Basic recipe for a rice soup (Congee) 4 cups / 500g. (rec.) - neutral - sweet... *
Basic recipe for a vegetable soup (nutritious) 2 cup / 500g. () - neutral - *....... *
Dulse (seaweed) 2 table spoons / 15g. () - neutral - salty .... water

Cooking instructions:
Worm up a portion of pre-cooked basic recipe for a ricesoup (congee) and a portion pre-cooked basic recipe for a vegetable soup.
Bake the dulse in the oven at 220 degrees for 3 minutes. Spread the crisp dulse over the rice.

9.29 Rice porridge with orange peel

Warms the stomach and spleen, harmonizes the intestine, forces Qi, reduces moisture. brings the Liver Qi in motion, cools heat, moisturizes, relaxes, builds up Qi, spreads. nourishes blood, moisturizes, relaxes, builds up Qi, spreads.
Cooking time approx. 10 min
Calories p. portion: 120
4 portions
Allergens: L

Quantity of ingredients:
Rice variety any 1 cup / 100g. (yes) - warm - sweet................................. metal
Water 6 cups / 600g. (yes) - cool - salty ....earth
Olive oil 1 table spoon / 10g. (yes) - cool - sweet.......................................earth
Champignon 1/2 cup / 50g. (rec.) - cool - sweet..earth
Celery sticks 1/2 bunch / 60g. (rec.) - cool - sweet....................................earth
Basic recipe for a chicken soup (warming) 3-4 table spoons / 40g. () - warm - **
Salt 1 pinch / 0,5g. (yes) - cold - salty .... water

Cooking instructions:

The day before boil the rice with the orange peel and water in a ratio of about 1: 6. The amount of water determines the thickness of the mash (pure matter of taste). Put the rice in a saucepan with good insulation and a heavy lid. It is important to simmer the rice after a short boil on the slightest flame, otherwise it burns. Boil the rice for 2-4 hours. The longer he cooks, the more he strengthens.

Heat the oil in a saucepan, add the chopped champignon and celery and sauté briefly. Add the rice. Add vegetable broth or water, warm up, salt.

9.30 Rice with parsnips

Regulates Qi, dries out, passes downwardly, warms the stomach and spleen, harmonizes the intestine, forces Qi, reduces moisture. moisturizes, relaxes, builds up Qi, spreads. distributes mucus, activates Wei Qi, forces Qi.
Cooking time approx. 45 min
Calories p. portion: 206
3 portions

Quantity of ingredients:

Rice variety any 1 cup / 120g. (yes) - warm - sweet.................................. metal
Water 1 1/2 cups / 200g. (yes) - cool - salty ....earth
Salt 1 pinch / 1g. (yes) - cold - salty .... water
Parsnip 3-4 pieces / 450g. (rec.) - cool - bitter ....fire
Olive oil 1 table spoon / 10g. (yes) - cool - sweet.......................................earth
Sage 1 teaspoon / 3g. (yes) - cool - bitter, spicy ....fire

Cooking instructions:

Peel the parsnips and cut into slices. Fry for a short time in oil. Add the rice and fry again for a short time. Add the water and cook it at least 30 min. Sprinkle with fresh chopped sage.

9.31 Rice with stewed vegetables

Dissipates heat and moisture.
Cooking time approx. 20 min
Calories p. portion: 166
2 portions
Allergens: L

Quantity of ingredients:
Rice variety any 1/2 cup / 60g. (yes) - warm - sweet................................. metal
Water 3 cups / 300g. (yes) - cool - salty..earth
Lemon peel 1 piece / 3g. (rec.) - cool - bitter..fire
Water 1/2 cup / 0g. (yes) - cool - salty...earth
Carrot 2 pieces / 180g. (yes) - neutral - sweet ....earth
Celery sticks 1/2 piece / 5g. (rec.) - cool - sweet.......................................earth
Champignon 1/2 cup / 50g. (rec.) - cool - sweet...earth
Cress 2 table spoons / 20g. (little) - cool - sweet.................................... metal
Linseed oil 1 dash / 3g. (rec.) - neutral - sweet ....earth

Cooking instructions:
Cook rice according to basic recipe with a piece of lemon peel.
Steam chopped carrots, celery and mushrooms until soft.
Then sprinkle with cress. Then add a dash of high quality cold oil.

9.32 Roasted millet with Celery sticks

Strengthens spleen and kidney, diuretic, brings the liver Qi in motion,
cools heat, moisturizes, relaxes, builds up Qi, spreads.
Cooking time approx. 30 min
Calories p. portion: 400
2 portions
Allergens: L

Quantity of ingredients:
Millet 1 cup / 120g. (yes) - cool - sweet, salty..earth
Water 1 1/2 cups / 240g. (yes) - cool - salty...earth
Celery sticks 2 rods / 50g. (rec.) - cool - sweet ....earth
Water 2 table spoons / 30g. (yes) - cool - salty ....earth
Salt 1 pinch / 1g. (yes) - cold - salty .... water
Sage 3-4 leaves / 2g. (yes) - cool - bitter, spicy ....fire
Cress 1 teaspoon / 3g. (little) - cool - sweet .... metal

Cooking instructions:
Roast millet briefly, pour over water, heat till it boils and let stand for 20
min. to swell.

Cut celery into small pieces and mix with water, salt and fresh herbs
and cook for 10 min. Add to the millet. Sprinkle fresh sage or
watercress over it.

9.33 Roasted millet with plum compote

Strengthens blood and fluids, regulates Qi, cools liver fire, produces humors, strengthens spleen and kidney, diuretic.
Cooking time approx. 30 min
Calories p. portion: 139
4 portions

Quantity of ingredients:
Millet 1 cup / 120g. (yes) - cool - sweet, salty...earth
Water 1 1/2 cups / 250g. (yes) - cool - salty..earth
Plum 1 1/2 cups / 250g. (little) - warm - sweet, sour .... wood
Vanilla pod 1 pinch / 1g. () - neutral - sweet..*
Water 5/8 lbs - 8oz / 250g. (yes) - cool - salty..earth
Cinnamon ground 1 pinch / 1g. (rec.) - hot - acrid, sweet................................*
Acerola fruit nectar or powder 1/2 teaspoon / 1g. () - warm - sour .... wood

Cooking instructions:
Roast millet briefly, pour over water, heat till it boils and let stand for 20 min. to swell.
Cook plums with water, vanilla and cinnamon 10 min. then strain. Add acerola and add to the millet.

9.34 Soup with cucumbers and tomatoes

Reduces damp heat, nourishes liver-Yin, cools heat, produces humors, calms nerves and stomach.
Cooking time approx. 10 min
Calories p. portion: 137
2 portions
Allergens: CO

Quantity of ingredients:
Cucumber 1 piece / 300g. (rec.) - cold - sweet...earth
Tomato 4 pieces (very ripe) / 200g. (rec.) - cold - sweet-sour.................. wood
Onion white 1 piece / 50g. (yes) - warm - acrid...metal
Peppers 1/2 piece (green) / 10g. (rec.) - cool - sweet ....earth
Salt 1 pinch / 0,5g. (yes) - cold - salty ....water
Vinegar (Apple vinegar) 1 dash / 2g. (little) - warm - sour, bitter .... wood
Water 1 cup / 120g. (yes) - cool - salty..earth
Chicken egg 2 pieces / 120g. (rec.) - neutral - sweet ....earth

Cooking instructions:
Puree all ingredients in the blender. Cool in the fridge. When serving, sprinkle with chopped breadcrumbs and finely chopped boiled egg.

9.35 Soup with egg yolk

Forces Qi and Yang, is very warming.
Cooking time approx. 5 min
Calories p. portion: 173
1 portion
Allergens: CO

Quantity of ingredients:
Basic recipe for a beef soup (warming) 5/8 lbs - 8oz / 250g. () - warm - *........ *
Chicken yolk 1 piece / 25g. (rec.) - neutral - sweet ....earth

Cooking instructions:
Warm the beef soup according to the basic recipe for a beef broth, warm it up and jell the yolk.

9.36 Spinach with Tahini

Nourishes blood and Yin, forces Zang-organs, forces stomach and intestines, harmonizes Qi, moisturizes lungs, forces Qi, forces spleen, relieves inflammation, moisturizes, relaxes, builds up Qi, spreads, nourishes blood.
Cooking time approx. 20 min
Calories p. portion: 150
4 portions
Allergens: N

Quantity of ingredients:
Potato 1,1 lbs / 500g. (yes) - neutral - sweet...earth
Salt 1 pinch / 0,2g. (yes) - cold - salty .... water
Water 1 cup / 25g. (yes) - cool - salty..earth
Spinach 2,2 lbs / 800g. (rec.) - cool - sweet, rough ....earth

Cooking instructions:
Cook potatoes and peel. Heat water. Blanch spinach. Shake off water and let it dry and stir with sesame.

9.37 Strawberry soup with melons

Forces blood, cools blood, preserves the fluids, contracts, moisturizes, spreads, forces heart Yin.
Cooking time approx. 5 min
Calories p. portion: 87
2 portions

Quantity of ingredients:
Strawberries 3/4 lbs / 300g. (rec.) - neutral - sweet, sour.......................... wood
Strawberry Juice 1/3 cup / 70g. (rec.) - neutral - sweet, sour................... wood
Lemon peel 1/4 teaspoon / 1g. (rec.) - cool - bitter......................................fire
Cantaloupe 5/8 oz / 200g. (rec.) - cold - sweet..earth

Cooking instructions:
Puree strawberries (fresh or frozen) and strawberry juice with the blender, mix in a little sugar. Cut melon pulp into small pieces. Arrange strawberry soup in portions. Put the melon cubes in the sweet soup.

9.38 Tea from basil

Dries out, passes downwardly.
Cooking time approx. 10 min
Calories p. portion: 0
4 portions

Quantity of ingredients:
Basil 1 teaspoon / 2g. (rec.) - warm - acrid, bitter .... fire
Water 2 cup / 500g. (yes) - cool - salty...earth

Cooking instructions:
Heat the water till it boils and put it aside. Add basil and 10 min. to let go. Sweet to taste with honey.

9.39 Tea from celery sticks

Brings the Liver Qi in motion, cools heat, moisturizes, relaxes, builds up Qi, spreads.
Cooking time approx. 15 min
Calories p. portion: 1
4 portions
Allergens: L

Quantity of ingredients:
Celery sticks 2 table spoons (chopped) / 18g. (rec.) - cool - sweet ....earth
Water 2 cup / 500g. (yes) - cool - salty...earth

Cooking instructions:
Heat the water till it boils and put it aside. Add cutted celery and cook for 10 min. to let go. Strain. Sweet to taste with honey.

9.40 Tea from cinnamon sticks

Warms the stomach and spleen, promotes blood circulation and conduction flow, relieves cold-sickness and pain.
Cooking time approx. 15 min
Calories p. portion: 2
1 portion

Quantity of ingredients:
Cinnamon sticks 1/4 piece / 1g. (rec.) - hot - acrid, sweet...............................*
Water 1 cup / 125g. (yes) - cool - salty..earth

Cooking instructions:
A quarter of a cinnamon stick for a cup of tea. Start cold and bring to the boil. Let it sit for 15 minutes, then strain.
This tea is unsweetened and swallowed, slowly drunk. The amount is enough for one day.

9.41 Tsampa with jam or fruit compote

Nourishes fluids, reduces stomach heat, forces spleen, produces essence, harmonizes stomach, moisturizes intestines.
Cooking time approx. 5 min
Calories p. portion: 280
1 portion
Allergens: AGO

Quantity of ingredients:
Tsampa 3 table spoons / 30g. (rec.) - cold - sweet, little salty...................earth
Water 6-8 table spoons / 70g. (yes) - cool - salty ....earth
Butter organic 1/2 teaspoon / 2g. (yes) - neutral - sweet...........................earth
Strawberry jam 1 table spoon / 7g. () - neutral - sweet, sour....................wood
Sunflower seeds 2 teaspoons / 14g. (rec.) - neutral - sweet ....earth
Apple (sweet) 1 piece grated / 120g. (yes) - cool - sweet, sour.................earth

Cooking instructions:
Pour Tsampa (roasted barley flour) with boiling water and stir with a spoon until a porridge is formed.
Add butter, jam, sunflower seeds and grated apple.
Sweet to taste with honey, whole cane sugar, or barley malt.
Spices and herbs: fresh mint, vanilla or cocoa, anise, cinnamon

Summer: jam or compote of your choice
Winter: nuts and apple or pear

9.42 Wheat fresh grain porridge with pears.

Moisturizes lungs, cools heat, reduces lung mucus, nourishes Yin from heart and kidney, forces heart and kidney, moisturizes, relaxes, builds up Qi, spreads.
Cooking time approx. 25 min
Calories p. portion: 309
2 portions
Allergens: ANO

Quantity of ingredients:
Wheat 1 cup / 100g. (rec.) - cool - sweet.. wood
Water 2-4 cups / 350g. (yes) - cool - salty..earth
Pear 2 pieces / 300g. (yes) - cool - sweet, sour ....earth
Raisins 1 table spoon / 10g. (little) - warm - sweet...................................earth
Sesame, white 1 table spoon / 8g. (yes) - neutral - sweet........................earth
Sunflower seeds 1 table spoon / 8g. (rec.) - neutral - sweet ....earth
Cardamom 1 pinch / 0,3g. () - warm - acrid.. metal
Salt 1 pinch / 0,3g. (yes) - cold - salty .... water

Cooking instructions:
Preparation the night before: Wheat roughly cut; soak overnight.

In the morning: Put the wheat meal with a little hot water; simmer with stirring for about 15 minutes.
Meanwhile, add pear compote, raisins, crushed sesame, sunflower seeds, some ground cardamom, a small pinch of salt.

Variants: with grated apple or seasonal fruit.

10 Effects of food

10.1 Use ingredients: recommendable

Agar agar (kelp)
Aloe juice
Artichoke
Asparagus (green or white)
Barley
Barley not peeled
Basic recipe for a duck soup
Basic recipe for a rice soup (Congee)
Basil
Basil (fresh)
Beef kidney
Berry juice
Blackberry´s
Blueberry
Boletus mushroom
Borage oil
Breadcrumbs (wheat bread, bread roll)
Brussels sprouts
Calamari
Cantaloupe
Carp
Celery root
Celery sticks
Champignon
Chanterelle
Chard
Cherry
Chicken egg
Chicken liver
Chicken yolk
Chicory
Cinnamon ground
Cinnamon sticks
Clove
Corn Grease (Polenta)
Cranberry
Cranberry juice
Cucumber
Duck (heart)
Duck (slaughtered)
Endive salad
Fish pieces mixed (fresh water)
French beans
Fruit tea
Gelée Royal
Grape juice red
Grape juice white
Grapes red
Grapes white

Herbs different varieties
Herbs of Provence
Herbs various
Herbs wild
Leaf salads (bitter)
Leek
Lemon peel
Lime
Linseed oil
Mediterranean fish (cod, plaice, haddock, sea eel, mackerel)
Morel, dried
Mulberry fruit
Mung bean
Mung bean sprouting
Okra
Oyster mushroom
Parsley
Parsnip
Peas
Peas, green
Peppers
Pigeon
Pork meat
Pumpkin seed oil
Pumpkin seeds
Quail
Quail egg
Quince
Radicchio
Raspberry
Raspberry dried (immature)
Reishi mushroom
Rice long grain rice
Rice noodles
Rice round grain
Rice wild (nature rice)
Sesame paste (Tahini)
Sesame, black
Shiitake, dried
Soybeans, black
Spinach
Strawberries
Strawberry Juice
Sunflower seeds
Tomato
Tomato dried
Tsampa (roasted barley flour)
Umeboshi plums (Japanese apricots)

Watermelon
Wheat
Wheat bran
Wheat bulgur
Wheat flakes

Wheat flour
Wheat semolina
Wheat semolina for children
Wild strawberries
Zucchini

10.2 Use ingredients: yes

Almond
Anchovy / Sardine
Apple (sour)
Apple (sweet)
Arrowroot
Balm
Bean oil
Bitter melon
Black-eyed peas
Blueberry juice
Broccoli
Buckwheat
Bulgur (cereals)
Butter organic
Carrot
Carrot (Early Carrot)
Carrot juice without sugar
Cashews
Cauliflower
Chinese cabbage
Clementines
Coconut grated
Cod
Coix (seeds) YiYi Ren
Cooking oil
Coriander
Corn
Couscous
Crème fraiche cheese
Currant (black)
Currant (red)
Currant (white)
Elderberry blossom tee
Evening primrose oil
Fennel
Fennel tea
Fig
Fig dried
Fish remains
Freshwater fish
Ginger oil
Goose
Goose parts
Gooseberry
Gourd
Hawthorn

Hazelnuts
Kefir
Kidney beans (red)
Kohlrabi
Lentils
Lentils black
Lentils red
Lentils yellow
Lychee
Lychee in Preserved
Mackerel
Mallow (Malva sylvestris) blossom tea
Malt
Maple syrup
Margarine
Margarine (diet)
Millet
Millet flakes
Morel (black, dried)
Mullet
Octopus
Olive oil
Olives
Onion (shallot)
Onion (spring onion)
Onion read
Onion white
Peanut oil
Peanuts
Pear
Pear juice
Perch
Pine nuts
Pinto beans speckled
Pistachios
Plaice
Pork heart
Pork knuckle
Pork liver
Pork skin
Pork stomach
Potato
Quinoa
Rabbit liver
Rabbit meat
Radish

Radish black
Rapeseed oil
Red cabbage
Rice (fragrance)
Rice (whole grain)
Rice Basmati
Rice black
Rice flour
Rice red
Rice sweet
Rice variety any
Rosefish
Rye
Rye flour
Saffron
Sage
Salmon
Salsify
Salt
Sauerkraut (cutted cabbage fermented)
Sesame oil
Sesame, white
Sorrel
Sour cherries
Soy flour
Soya Cuisine (soy cream)

Soybean milk
Soybeans
Soybeans, yellow
Spelled (Dark) bread
Spelled flakes
Spelled grain
Spelled semolina
Spelled wholemeal flour
Sugar molasses
Sunflower oil
Sweet potato
Tangerine
Thistle oil
Trout
Turmeric (yellow root)
Vanilla
Vanilla powder
Vegetable juice
Walnut oil
Walnuts
Water
Water hot
Wheat germ oil
White bread (wheat bread)
Wild boar meat

10.3 Use ingredients: little

Adzuki beans
Almond marzipan
Almond milk
Almond puree
Amaranth
Anise (Common Fennel)
Apricot
Apricots
Aubergine
Bamboo shoots
Batavia
Beef bone marrow
Beef fillet
Beef heart
Beef liver
Beef lungs (calf)
Beef meat
Beef meat (calf)
Beef meatbones
Beef stomach
Black beans
Broad beans (thick beans)
Burdock root tea
Bush beans

Butter beans white
Carambola (Star fruit)
Caviar
Cherry juice
Chestnuts
Chicken heart
Chicken meat
Chicken stomach
Chickpeas
Coconut flakes
Coconut milk
Cow's milk (1.5% fat)
Cow's milk (whole milk 3.5% fat)
Cress
Cumin (Caraway seed)
Dandelion (young plants)
Dandelionroots tea
Dates dried
Deer meat
Dill
Fresh cheese
Grapefruit (Pomelo)
Grapefruit juice
Green spelt

Honey
Iceberg lettuce
Kiwi
Lady's mantle
Lamb's lettuce
Lettuce
Lima beans
Longane
Mango
mango powder
Mold cheese
Mozzarella
Multi-grain bread (gray bread)
Oat
Oat flakes (whole grain)
Oat flakes roasted
Oat flour
Oat fusion (baby food)
Oat meal
Oat milk
Oysters
Papaya
Parmesan
Peaches
Peaches (canned)
Pheasant
Plum

Pomegranate
Pumpkin
Radish (white, green, purple-red)
Raisins
Rhubarb
Rice malt
Romaine lettuce / lettuce salad
Rose hip tea
Sago (cereals)
Sour milk cheese 20%
Soybean oil
Sugar brown
Sugar candy white
Sugar cane sugar
Sugar fructose - fruit sugar
Sugar glucose - grapes sugar
Sugar Milk Sugar
Sugar white
Turkey breast meat
Vinegar (Apple vinegar)
Vinegar (Red wine vinegar)
Vinegar Aceto Balsamico
White beans
Yarrow tea
Yogurt (natural, 1.5% fat)
Yogurt (natural, 3.5% fat)

10.4 Do not use contra-acting foods

Avocado
Banana
Banana (cooking banana)
Beer (Pils)
Beer (Top-fermented German dark beer)
Black caraway
Black tea
Boxhorn clover seeds
Buttermilk
Cereal coffee
Chili (pod or ground)
Chives
Chlorella (fresh water)
Cocoa
Coffee
Crab
Cream, sweet 30%
Curd cheese 20%
Curd cheese 40%
Curry
Curry paste red
Deer meat
Eel

Feta cheese
Garlic
Ginger fresh
Ginger powder
Goat
Goat and sheep's milk
Goat cheese
Goose egg
Green tea
Ground
Ground caraway
Hyssop
Juniper berry
Kombu seaweed (Saccharina japonica)
Kumquats
Lamb bones
Lamb kidneys
Lamb liver
Lamb meat
Lamb shoulder
Lemon
Lemon juice
Lobster
Lovage

Marjoram
Mineral water
Miso paste (soy bean paste)
Mussels
Mustard seeds
Mutton
Mutton
Nutmeg
Orange
Orange juice
Oregano dried
Pepper Cayenne
Pepper white (ground)
Peppercorns
Pepperoni, red, pitted, halved
Peppers (rose peppers)
Pimento
Pineapple
Pineapple (from a can)
Pineapple juice without sugar
Poppy
Rabbit

Red wine
Rosemary
Sake
Seacrab
Sheep's milk
Shrimp
Sour cream (Schmand) 30% fat
Sour cream 15% fat
Sour milk
Soy sauce
Soy Tofu
Spiny lobsters
Spirit
Star anise
Tarragon (Estragon)
Thyme
Tuna
Wakame
Wheat beer
White wine
Wormwood
Yogi tea

11 Complementary

11.1 Blueberries leaves

Myrtillus, fruct., Myrtillus, fol.
Preparation: Healing tea (infusion)
Guides damp-heat from the intestines, supports spleen-qi, drains
moisture-heat from the bladder, supports kidney-qi and bladder-Qi.
Dosage: 5-10g leaves on 1 liter of water.

11.2 Dead-nettles

Lamium album, herb.
Preparation: Healing tea (infusion)
Astringent in the lower heater, tonifies kidney-qi and spleen-qi, clears
damp- heat in the abdomen. Dissipating and cooling in bladder and
intestines. Cools Kidney-Yin and Heart-Yin.
Dosage: Pour 3 teaspoons of blossoms and cabbage with ¼ liter of
boiling water, infuse for 5 minutes and strain. Drink 3 cups of it daily.

11.3 Fennel

Foeniculum vulgare
Preparation: Healing tea (infusion)

Strengthens the stomach energy, warms kidney energy and has an energizing effect.

For the powder, roast the fennel in a dry pan until it starts to smell, then grind it to a fine powder in a mortar or food processor; Add 1-5 g powder with boiling water and drink daily.

Special Features: Fennel is one of the best remedy for physical weakness and lack of vitality due to inadequate or cold digestive energy that prevents that the body absorbs enough nutrients and energy from food.

Dosage: Pour 3-5 grams of tea over with 250 ml of boiling water and leave for 10 minutes. Then sieve. Drink in three doses on an empty stomach

Note: In rare cases, skin, stomach and intestinal reactions were observed. Active ingredients: essential oil, trans-anethole, fenchone, fatty oil, protein, sugar.

11.4 Juniper berries

Juniperus, fruct.

Preparation: Decoction

Dries out, heads down, activates Wei Qi. Relieves wind moisture and transforms. Tonifies Spleen-Qi, Stomach-Qi, Heart-Qi, Kidney-Qi and Kidney-Yang, warms the inside. Guides moisture and heat out of the bladder.

Use: tea, season

Dosage: Pour 2 teaspoons of the tea into 250 ml of boiling water and leave for 10 minutes. Then sieve. Drink 2 to 3 cups per day as needed.

Note: Avoid overdose, pregnant women and acute kidney patients should do without. External rubbing may cause blistering of the skin.

12 Basics of Nutrition

The basic principles of nutrition described herein are general recommendations. They are not aimed at a specific form of therapy. Recommendations concerning a therapy have priority.

12.1 Nutrition

Regular meals in a relaxed atmosphere. A warm breakfast is considered a good start into the day.
The main meals ought to be taken for lunch – supper in the early evening. Pay attention to feeling hungry or sated: don't eat too much nor remain hungry is the rule
Prepare the meals freshly from natural, regional products. Frozen, heat-conserved, industrially prepared or foodstuffs cooked in the microwave oven are rejected.
Choice of foodstuffs according to the season: more cooling food in summer, more warming food in winter.
Eat cooked food at least twice a day. Food and drinks ought to be lukewarm, never ice-cold or hot.
Raw vegetables, briefly cooked vegetables, freshly squeezed juices and mineral water are not recommended. Milk and dairy products are only included in the diet if they don't cause problems.
Don't use therapeutic recipes over a longer period without consulting your doctor or therapist.

Varied food
Enjoy the diversity of foodstuffs. Characteristics of a balanced nutrition are variety, suitable combination and a balanced quantity of rich and low energy foodstuffs (on one hand avoiding undersupply with essential nutrients and on the other hand to take to many undesirable substances).

A lot of Cereal Products - and Potatoes
Bread, pasta, rice, cereal flakes (best wholemeal) as well as potatoes contain almost no fat, but many vitamins, mineral nutrients, trace elements, roughage and secondary plant substances. These foodstuffs ought to be taken with low-fat side dishes.

Vegetables and Fruit – „Take Five" every day ...
5 portions of vegetables and fruit a day, as fresh as possible, briefly cooked, or maybe one portion as a juice – ideal as a side dish to every meal as well as snack between meals: Thus a lot of vitamins, mineral nutrients as well as roughage and secondary plant substances

Daily milk and dairy products
Milk and Dairy Products every Day, once or twice per Week Fish; meat, sausages as well as eggs moderately. These foodstuffs contain valuable nutrients like calcium in the milk, iodine selenium and omega-3 fat acids in saltwater fish. Meat is favorable due to its high content of disposable iron and the vitamins B1, B6 and B12. Quantities of 300 – 600 g meat and sausage per week are sufficient. Prefer low-fat products, especially in meat- and dairy products.

Low-fat and fatty Foodstuffs
Fat supplies us with essential fat acids and fatty foodstuffs contain also fat-soluble vitamins. Fat is high in energy; therefore much fat in the food may cause overweight, possibly also cancer. Too many saturated fat acids may further a tendency for cardio-vascular diseases in the long term. Prefer vegetable oils and fats (e.g. rapeseed-, olive-, soya-oils and solid fats produced therefrom). Beware of invisible fat in meat- and dairy products, pastry and sweets as well as in fast-food and convenience foods. 70 – 90 g fat per day is sufficient.

Moderately Sugar and Salt
Take sugar and foods/drinks containing various kinds of sugar (e.g. glucose syrup) only occasionally. Use herbs and spices as well as a little salt creatively. Prefer salt containing iodine.

Plenty of Liquids
Water is absolutely essential. Drink 1-2 l liquids every day. Prefer water (with or without gas) and other low-calorie drinks. Alcoholic drinks should not be taken.

Tasty Dishes, carefully cooked
Cook the meals with as low temperatures and as short as possible, using little water and fat – this preserves the original taste, keeps the nutrients intact and prevents the production of harmful compounds.

Take time and enjoy the food
Take your Time and enjoy your Food
Eating consciously helps to eat right. The eye enjoys food, too. It's fun, invites to enjoy varied dishes and stimulates the feeling of satiety.

Watch your Weight and stay in Motion
A balanced diet and a lot of exercise and sport (30 – 60 min/day) are a healthy combination. The right weight furthers well-being and health. Thermals, directional effectiveness, digestive power

There are various criteria for judging the effectiveness of herbs and foodstuffs.

The use of certain herbs and ingredients is based on observations of the effects on the body which these foodstuffs, herbs and spices show after having eaten them. The medical science has developed following system: Every ingredient or herb has a directional effectiveness. Furthermore, there are herbs which have a special effect on certain organs.

The basic condition for a healthy metabolism is to obtain sufficient energy from food and that the digestive process doesn't use too much energy. An easily digestible meal makes content and sated, doesn't cause flatulence and fatigue after the meal. The perfect spices increase the healthiness of our meals. Very often, just small doses of herbs and spices will suffice. They are not used to make us sated, but to help our digestive organs to digest the food.

12.2 Recipes

The recipes list the ingredients to be used and the cooking instructions show how the dish is prepared. The list of ingredients shows the concerned quantities as well as the relevance for the therapy. If you find „less than mentioned", try to comply or find an alternative from the „list of recommended foodstuffs". Mostly it shall result just in a small change of taste when you simply avoid this ingredient.

Mild cooking methods: boiling, stewing, poaching, steaming
Strong cooking methods: barbecuing, roasting, frying, smoking
Balanced cooking methods: deep-frying, baking brick
Deep-freezing and warming in the microwave oven should be avoided (denaturalization).

12.3 Foodstuffs

Foodstuffs have an effect on body and soul like medicinal herbs, only a very much milder one. Dietary advice is mainly based on regional foodstuffs. The knowledge about the effects of each foodstuff and the knowledge, when which foodstuff shall be used, is based on the orthodox school of medicine. Use ecologic-organic products, if possible. As everything should be cooked for a long time due to a better digestability and very rarely eaten raw, the food agrees with everyone.

The classification of the foodstuffs according to their effect on the body is the basis in order to achieve a harmonious status of health.

Dietary advisors do not recommend certain foodstuffs for everyone. The individual diet is tailor-made for the individual constitution.

Buy only fresh and ripe fruit and vegetables. You ought to leave unripe fruit and vegetables and such with brown spots and wilted leaves behind in the market. In this case take deep-frozen goods (never ready-to-serve dishes!). Fruit and vegetables are deep-frozen immediately after harvesting and often contain more vitamins and minerals than the goods from the vegetable shelf. Whereas conserved or tinned goods contain very much less biological substances. Also, salt, sugar and others are mostly added to the latter. Never leave the foodstuffs in the water after washing them to avoid that many vital substances get drowned. Clean salads, fruit and vegetables immediately before serving.

Please make sure of the hygienic processing of foodstuffs. Clean your salads, fruit and vegetables carefully. When cooking with meat, prepare all ingredients first and then process the meat products. Clean the worktop and tools very carefully. Wooden surfaces ought to be treated with a mild disinfectant regularly in order to reduce germination.

Store fruit and vegetables separately, if possible. Harvested fruit and vegetables are still alive and emit e.g. ethylene gas, which makes other products ripen and age faster. Keep meat and fish in the closed packaging or store them in the fridge in closed containers.

12.4 Herbs

There are some basic rules for storing medicinal herbs. On principle, herbs must be protected from direct sunlight, humidity and heat.

Containers for the storage of herbs may be glasses, ceramic jars and even plastic containers. However, plastic is a rather unsuitable material and should only be a short-term solution. In case of glass containers, use a dark material.

Medicinal herbs cannot be kept for any long period. The shelf life of herbs is limited. However, it can be prolonged with suitable storage. The place should be dark, rather cool and absolutely dry. A wooden medicine cabinet, placed not directly next to a source of heat, would be ideal. Never buy large quantities of herbs so as not to have to throw them away. Label the container with the name of the herb and the date of harvesting or processing.

13 Other dietic-books

The following syndromes of dietetics, TCM or for a therapy supplement for cancer are available.

Dietetics

E001. Nutrition of the infant - baby food
E002. Nutrition during lactation
E003. Nutrition in old age
E004. Nutrition of children and adolescents
E005. Nutrition of athletes
E006. Light weight
E007. Pregnancy
E008. Full food

Protein and electrolyte - kidneys
E009. (hemodialysis) dialysis treatment
E010. Acute renal failure
E011. Chronic renal insufficiency
E012. Nephrotic syndrome
E013. Kidney stones (nephrolithiasis)

Gastrointestinal tract - pancreas
E014. Acute pancreatitis (inflammation of the pancreas)
E015. Chronic pancreatitis (inflammation of the pancreas)

Gastrointestinal tract - small intestine and large intestine
E016. Acute obstipation (constipation)
E017. Chronic obstipation (constipation)
E018. Colon irritabile
E019. Diverticulitis
E020. Acquired lactose intolerance (lactose malabsorption)
E021. Fructose malabsorption
E022. Glutensensitive enteropathy (celiac disease)
E023. Colectomy
E024. Short Bowel Syndrome

Gastrointestinal tract - liver, gallbladder, bile ducts
E025. Acute and chronic hepatitis (inflammation of the liver)
E026. Cholelithiasis (bile stones)
E027. fatty liver
E028. cirrhosis

Gastrointestinal tract - Stomach and duodenal intestine
E029. Acute gastritis
E030. Chronic gastritis
E031. Stomach bleeding
E032. Ulcus ventriculi and duodenal ulcer
E033. Condition after gastric surgery

Gastrointestinal tract - oral cavity and esophagus
E034. Stomatitis
E035. Esophageal carcinoma (esophageal cancer)
E036. Refluosophagitis (heartburn)

Special diseases
E037. Phenylketonuria (PKU)
E038. Rheumatic joint diseases

Metabolism
E039. Obesity (overweight)
E040. Diabetes mellitus
E041. Eating disorders (underweight)

Fat metabolism
E042. Hypercholesterolaemia (increased cholesterol level)
E043. Hepatic Encephalopathy

Heart and circulation
E044. Arteriosclerosis (arterial calcification)
E045. Heart insufficiency
E046. Hypertension
E047. Hyperuricaemia and gout

Changed nutrient requirements
E048. In case of fever
E049. For malignant diseases
E050. After burns
E051. Radiation and chemotherapy

CANCER
E100. Pancreatic cancer
E101. Bladder cancer
E102. Blood cancer (leukemia)
E103. Breast cancer
E104. Colorectal cancer
E105. Gastric cancer
E106. Kidney cancer
E107. Esophageal cancer

TCM
E200. Bladder - moisture heat in the bladder
E201. Bladder - moisture and cold in the bladder
E202. Bladder - emptiness and cold in the bladder
E203. Large intestine - external cold affects the large intestine
E204. Large intestine - moisture heat in the large intestine
E205. Large intestine - heat blocks the intestine II acute
E206. Large intestine - dryness of the colon
E207. Large intestine - Yang deficiency (cold)
E208. Heart - Blood insufficiency
E209. Heart - Blood stagnation
E210. Heart - Fire
E211. Heart - Hot mucus clogs the heart pores

E212. Heart - Cold mucus clogs the heart pores
E213. Heart - Qi deficiency
E214. Heart - Yang deficiency
E215. Heart - Yin deficiency
E216. Liver - Ascending Liver Yang
E217. Liver - Blood deficiency
E218. Liver - Blood stagnation
E219. Liver - Moisture heat in liver and gall bladder
E220. Liver - Fire
E221. Liver - Gall bladder Qi-Empty
E222. Liver - Cold in the liver meridian
E223. Liver - Qi stagnation
E224. Liver - Wind
E225. Liver - Wind with ascending liver Yang
E226. Liver - Wind with blood anemic
E227. Liver - Wind with extreme heat
E228. Lung - Qi deficiency
E229. Lung - Mucus-moisture in the lungs
E230. Lung - Mucus-heat in the lungs
E231. Lung - Mucus-cold in the lungs
E232. Lung - Dryness of the lungs
E233. Lung - Wind-heat attacks the lungs
E234. Lung - Wind-cold affects the lungs
E235. Lung - Yin deficiency
E236. Stomach - Bloodstagnation
E237. Stomach - Fire
E238. Stomach - Cold with liquid
E239. Stomach - Nutrition stagnation
E240. Stomach - Qi deficiency
E241. Stomach - Rebellious Qi
E242. Stomach - Yin Emptiness
E243. Spleen - Heat and moisture attack the spleen
E244. Spleen - Coldness and moisture affects the spleen
E245. Spleen - Qi deficiency
E246. Spleen - Qi deficiency + Declining spleen Qi
E247. Spleen - Qi deficiency + spleen does not control the blood
E248. Spleen - Yang deficiency
E249. Kidney - Heart and kidney no longer communicate
E250. Kidney - Jing deficiency
E251. Kidney - Kidneys cannot receive the Qi
E252. Kidney - Qi is not stable
E253. Kidney - Yang deficiency
E254. Kidney - Yin deficiency

For further information visit di-book.com.

14 EBNS - Software for nutritional counseling

The main task of the database is to create personalized nutritional advice for each patient individually. The database was developed for Dietetics and Traditional Chinese Medicine.

The Database supports training and advices in the daily work routine.

The computer program provides lists of recipes, ingredients and herbs, which are given to the client. individually adjustable according to patient's request from whole food to vegetarians (lacto, ovo, ...). For every register there is an information sheet which can be given to the client. All texts can be individually designed.

The syndromes can be combined and result in an intersection of the recommended recipes and ingredients. The automated diagnosis for the TCM enables you to check your experience during the training as well as to confirm your diagnosis in the working day. You select several predefined symptoms and have the program automatically display the relevant syndromes.

How to work with the database:
Select the patient / client, select one or more of the syndromes you diagnosed and print the folder.

You can change all values, create new symptoms or syndromes, develop recipes, change or adapt ingredients and herbs to your findings. In simple client management, all relevant data about the person is stored. You get an overview of the past diagnoses and the development of the course of the disease.

As a consultant you save a lot of time when you print out the recipe, food and herbal lists for the recognized syndromes and give them to the clients. You can use this time for a personal conversation. With the database, dieticians and nutritionists can view the nutrients and trace elements for each recipe and develop recipes for syndromes even with suggested ingredients.

All recipe and grocery lists can also be ordered from me as a combination of several diseases. I wish all readers good luck, health and happiness in life.
More information can be found at www.ebns.at.
Volunteer: www.krebsinfo.at
Josef Miligui